Ecosystems Research Journal

Mississippi River Research Journal

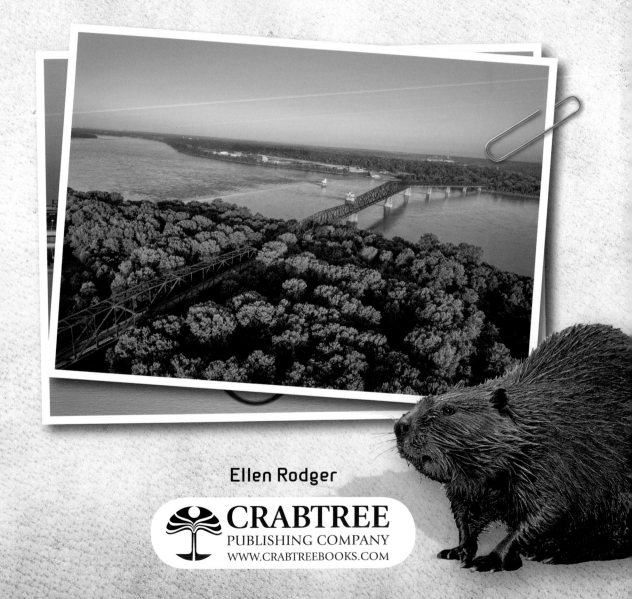

Ellen Rodger

CRABTREE
PUBLISHING COMPANY
WWW.CRABTREEBOOKS.COM

CRABTREE
PUBLISHING COMPANY
WWW.CRABTREEBOOKS.COM

Author: Ellen Rodger

Editors: Sonya Newland, Kathy Middleton

Design: Clare Nicholas

Cover design: Abigail Smith

Proofreader: Wendy Scavuzzo

**Production coordinator and
prepress technician:** Tammy McGarr

Print coordinator: Katherine Berti

Produced for Crabtree Publishing Company
by White-Thomson Publishing

Photo Credits:

Cover: All images from Shutterstock

Interior: Alamy: p. 12r Lyroky, p. 13l ZUMA Press, Inc., pp. 16–17 Nature and Science, p. 17t Jim West, p. 18r moris kushelevitch, p. 19t For Alan, p. 21t Goss Images; iStock: p. 10b RiverNorthPhotography, p. 15t twphotos, p. 22r AngelMcNallphotography, p. 25b mashuk, p. 28 marekuliasz; Shutterstock: pp. 4–5 Joseph Sohm, p. 5 Paul Brady Photography, p. 6l Tomaz Kunst, p. 6r Morphart Creation, p.7t Christian Musat, p. 7b Jay Stuhlmiller, p. 8 Steve Quinlan, p. 9t Krasowit, p. 9m Dn Br, p. 9b marekuliasz, pp. 10–11 Martin Michael Rudlof, p. 11t H. Häring, p. 11b Gregory Johnston, p.12l Vladimir Wrangel, p. 13r Jurand, p. 14 Burrhead64, p.15bl Preston james Garbe, p. 15br, p. 16b Mark tegges, p. 17b MadBird Illustrations, p. 18l KennStilger47, p. 19b Montypeter, p. 20l fishvector, pp. 20–21 IrinaK, p.21b Shackleford Photography, p. 22l Thorsten Grohse, p.23t Donald T. Devine, p.23b Wyatt Rivard, p.24t Zack Frank, p. 24b Madeleine Openshaw, p. 25t Warren Price Photography, p. 26l romarti, p. 26r Sam Spicer, p. 27t Mark Winfrey, p. 27b meunierd, p. 29t Gerald Marella, p. 29b Igor Kovalenko.

Library and Archives Canada Cataloguing in Publication

Rodger, Ellen, author
    Mississippi River research journal / Ellen Rodger.

(Ecosystems research journal)
Includes index.
Issued in print and electronic formats.
ISBN 978-0-7787-4659-1 (hardcover).--
ISBN 978-0-7787-4672-0 (softcover).--
ISBN 978-1-4271-2063-2 (HTML)

    1. Mississippi River--Juvenile literature. 2. Biotic communities--Mississippi River--Juvenile literature. 3. Stream ecology--Mississippi River--Juvenile literature. 4. Ecology--Mississippi River--Juvenile literature. I. Title.

QH104.5.M5R63 2018   j577.6'40977   C2017-907619-1
                                                                   C2017-907620-5

Library of Congress Cataloging-in-Publication Data

CIP Available at the Library of Congress

Crabtree Publishing Company

www.crabtreebooks.com   1-800-387-7650

Printed in the U.S.A./022018/CG20171220

Published in Canada
Crabtree Publishing
616 Welland Ave.
St. Catharines, Ontario
L2M 5V6

Published in the United States
Crabtree Publishing
PMB 59051
350 Fifth Avenue, 59th Floor
New York, New York 10118

Published in the United Kingdom
Crabtree Publishing
Maritime House
Basin Road North, Hove
BN41 1WR

Published in Australia
Crabtree Publishing
3 Charles Street
Coburg North
VIC, 3058

Contents

Mission to the Mississippi River

My bags are packed and I'm ready to roll on the river. The Mississippi River, that is. This is a trip of a lifetime. I'm a limnologist. Limnologists are scientists who study rivers, lakes, and streams. A conservation group called Big River Protection Network has asked me to write a report on the health of the Mississippi River. I will follow the river from its source in Minnesota to its end at the Gulf of Mexico. Along the way, I will record information on water quality, animals, and plants. I will look for signs of environmental damage. I will also gather information on how river **habitats** have changed.

Mississippi watershed

The Mississippi's watershed includes parts of 31 states in the United States and 2 provinces in Canada.

The Mississippi is the second-longest river in the United States. It is measured at 2,320 to 2,552 miles long depending on the year and how it is measured. I plan to visit forests, swamps, and wildlife **refuges**. The river has an enormous watershed. A watershed is an area of land that catches rain and snow and drains into a river. The Mississippi is a major transportation route for shipping goods. It also provides drinking water for 18 million people and water for agriculture. But human activities are having an impact on the river.

The Middle and Upper Mississippi meet at the city of St. Louis in Missouri.

Upper Mississippi: Headwaters to St. Louis, Missouri

Middle Mississippi: St. Louis, Missouri, to Cairo, Illinois

Lower Mississippi: Cairo, Illinois, where the Ohio River flows into the Mississippi River, to the Gulf of Mexico

Field Journal: Days 1–13

Lake Itasca, Minnesota

The Big River Protection Network has provided a support team to help me with my research. Today, we traveled to Lake Itasca State Park in Minnesota. This is where the Mississippi River begins. The starting place of a river is called its headwaters. The Mississippi starts as a slow-moving stream. It is so shallow we could walk across it on a group of rocks. From here, it flows northward, then winds its way east and south. Long ago, loggers cut down the pine forests on the river's edge. Today, the trees are preserved. Tree roots hold onto the soil and keep the river banks from **eroding**.

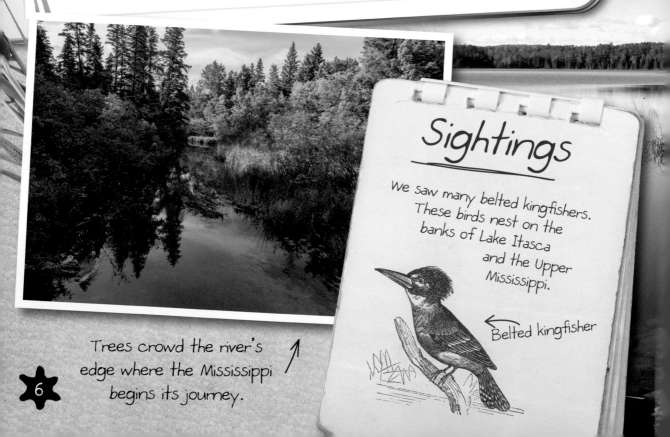

Sightings

We saw many belted kingfishers. These birds nest on the banks of Lake Itasca and the Upper Mississippi.

← Belted kingfisher

Trees crowd the river's edge where the Mississippi begins its journey. ↑

We launched canoes in the shallow waters of the river. Sometimes, we brushed the bottom as we paddled. The water is only 3 feet (0.9 meters) deep in some places. The river here has several paths, called channels. They are littered with dead trees. I noted a few beaver dams. That's good news! Beavers are important to the river environment. The dams that they build improve the water habitat by slowing the flow of water and creating a pond. Soil settles to the bottom of the pond and helps plants such as lily pads grow. Many fish, birds, and other animals come to feed on the plants. When the plants die, they decay and break down harmful chemicals in the water.

Beaver ↑

Lake Itasca is a "kettle lake." When **glaciers** moved along the ground, they dug into it. They left holes called kettles that filled with water when the ice melted.

Lake Itasca

7

Field Journal: Days 14–15

Minneapolis and Saint Paul, Minnesota

As we paddled, we noticed that the riverbanks became easier to see. Instead of marshes and grasses, there was clear shoreline. The water also got deeper the farther we traveled. Other rivers flow into the Mississippi as it flows south. These rivers are called tributaries. Tributary rivers add more water, making the Mississippi wider and faster. Near Minneapolis and Saint Paul, dams and locks were built in the 1900s to make it easier for ships to travel up or down the river. The dams lower and raise the water. They also interrupt the river's natural flow. Dams change the floodplain—the area surrounding the river that would normally flood each year.

lock

river

canal

↑ There are 29 locks on the Upper Mississippi River. They are connected by canals.

Major Mississippi Tributaries

Recorded river lengths change depending on when and how they are measured.

River	Length
Arkansas River	1,460 miles (2,349 kilometers)
Illinois River	273 miles (439 kilometers)
Missouri River	2,540 miles (4,088 kilometers)
Ohio River	1,310 miles (2,108 kilometers)

0   500   1,000 1,500 2,000 2,500
length

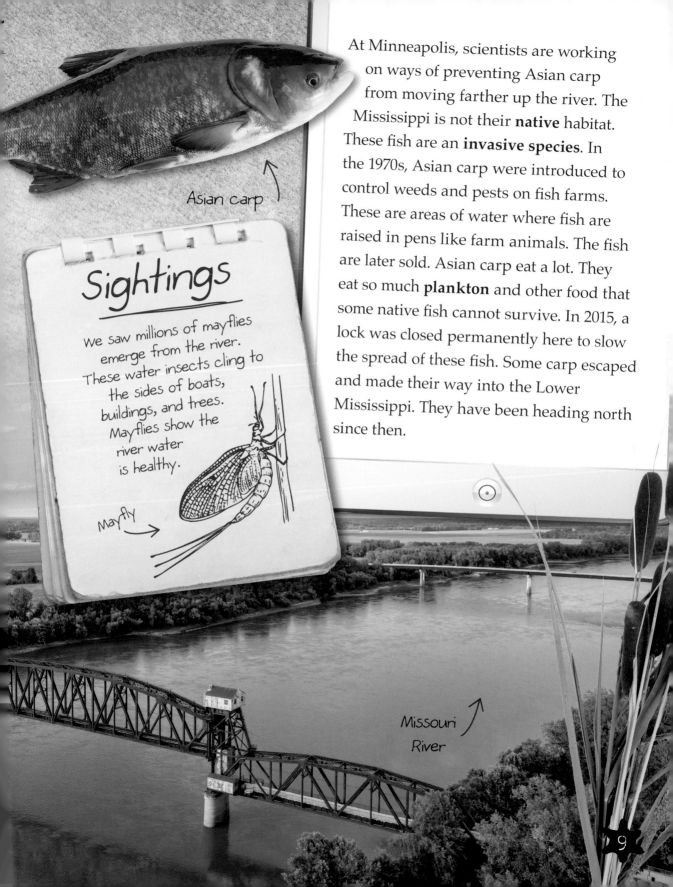

Asian carp

At Minneapolis, scientists are working on ways of preventing Asian carp from moving farther up the river. The Mississippi is not their **native** habitat. These fish are an **invasive species**. In the 1970s, Asian carp were introduced to control weeds and pests on fish farms. These are areas of water where fish are raised in pens like farm animals. The fish are later sold. Asian carp eat a lot. They eat so much **plankton** and other food that some native fish cannot survive. In 2015, a lock was closed permanently here to slow the spread of these fish. Some carp escaped and made their way into the Lower Mississippi. They have been heading north since then.

Sightings

We saw millions of mayflies emerge from the river. These water insects cling to the sides of boats, buildings, and trees. Mayflies show the river water is healthy.

Mayfly →

Missouri River ↗

Upper Mississippi National Wildlife & Fish Refuge

Today, we put our kayaks on our truck and drove to the Upper Mississippi River National Wildlife & Fish Refuge. We scanned the sky for birds. The forest refuge is on a floodplain, which is flat land that is sometimes under water. An American white pelican flew above us. This is one of the largest birds in North America. Flocks of pelicans sometimes work together to herd fish to the river's shore. Then they scoop them up into their huge bills.

American white pelicans

The Upper Mississippi River National Wildlife & Fish Refuge is located in four states: Minnesota, Wisconsin, Iowa, and Illinois. It covers 240,000 acres (97,125 hectares) —around 261 miles (420 kilometers) of river.

Upper Mississippi River
NATIONAL WILDLIFE & FISH REFUGE

U.S. Fish and Wildlife Service
Department of the Interior

In Cooperation With Minnesota Department of Transportation
Lower I-90 Landing

Locks and dams have changed water levels on the river. This has led to the erosion of river islands. Erosion makes the water thick and muddy, making it hard for sunlight to reach the bottom. Without sunlight, water plants can't grow. With no plants to eat, there are no fish and water birds. One solution to the problem is to collect **sediment** from the river bottom with a **dredge** to build new islands. We were invited to examine some new islands built by the Capoli Slough Habitat Rehabilitation Project. We could see birds already using the islands to nest.

I caught a glimpse of an American mink swimming near the islands. Another good sign!

natstat STATUS REPORT ST456/part B

Name: Great blue heron
(Ardea herodias)

Description:
A long-legged bird, the blue heron stalks and eats fish, frogs, and turtles. It has a wingspan up to 6 feet (1.8 meters) wide. Great blue herons make their nests, called rookeries, in treetops on the banks of the river.

Attach photograph here →

Threats:
Predators, such as bald eagles, destroy nests and eat eggs. **Herbicides** from farming and chemicals from industry seep into the river and poison the heron's food sources.

Numbers:
Unknown

Status:
Least concern

Field Journal: Days 18–19

Dubuque to Davenport, Iowa

Like a lot of places on the Mississippi, Davenport is prone to flooding from April to July. As winter ice melts in the Upper Mississippi, the water flows downstream. The river's vast watershed means water from dozens of rivers and streams flows into the river, too. Rain that trickles into a river in the Rocky Mountains can make its way to the Mississippi. All this adds up. **Global warming** is changing weather, creating more storms and heavier rainfall in spring. Spring and early summer are the flood seasons on the Mississippi River.

After a major flood in Iowa in 1965, Dubuque built a floodwall and gates to protect the city. These kept the city safe during a record flood in 1995.

I saw a spotted gar in the waters here.

Floods in Davenport

Davenport uses sandbags stacked on top of each other instead of permanent levees to prevent flooding. Levees are high embankments on the sides of the river. They prevent the river from overflowing. A wall that surrounds a baseball park on Davenport's riverbank acts like a levee. The wall is removable and prevents floodwaters from entering the park and surrounding area.

Sandbags

Flooding is a fact of life on the Mississippi. After a major flood in 1993, Davenport decided to remove some buildings near the river front instead of building a levee.

The Davenport baseball park floodwall was built in 2011. It is made from aluminum panels that are 10 feet (3 meters) long, 4 inches (10 centimeters) wide, and 8 feet (2.4 meters) high.

13

Field Journal: Days 20–2

Missouri River Towns to St. Louis

We're on a road trip! And we've become pros at bird watching. The Mississippi River is part of a major bird **migration** route called the Mississippi Flyway. It is one of four flyways in North America. Birds follow these flight paths every year. The many forests, wetlands, and grasslands on the Mississippi River are where birds rest and feed. Migrating birds stop here on their way to and from the Gulf of Mexico to nesting areas in Canada.

More than 325 species use the flyway, including whooping cranes, warblers, and brown pelicans. About 40 percent of North America's waterfowl migrate along this route.

Snow geese are just one of more than 300 species that can be seen migrating along the Mississippi Flyway.

Today, we met with volunteers from the Trumpeter Swan Society. They monitor and protect this bird that was once almost **extinct**. We helped put new neck collars and leg bands on some swans. The bands help the society track where the birds are living. The good news is that the swan population is recovering from 100 years of overhunting. The bad news is that climate change is a new threat to their health and habitat. Climate change is an increased warming of Earth's atmosphere. It is caused when a gas called carbon dioxide traps the Sun's heat near Earth.

In the 1900s, hunters killed trumpeter swans for their feathers. They were used as decorations on hats.

Part of the Mississippi runs through Tornado Alley. This is an area where tornados are frequent events. They've become more frequent with global warming.

Sightings

I spotted a Eurasian tree sparrow. These birds were imported from Germany in the late 1800s. About 15,000 of them make their home here now.

Eurasian tree sparrow

Field Journal: Days 23–25

Middle Mississippi River National Wildlife Refuge

Today, we visited the Middle Mississippi River National Wildlife Refuge. The refuge is in the river's floodplain in the states of Illinois and Missouri. Birds that live along the water find food in the channels off the river. These channels are important areas for fish, such as black crappie, white bass, and channel catfish, to lay their eggs. We paddled by woods of cottonwood, pecan, and sycamore trees. Tree roots help prevent riverbanks from falling into the river. They also give bald eagles a place to nest and hunt.

The refuge is on land that was flooded in the Great Mississippi Flood of 1993. Some of the land was flooded for over 200 days.

I heard the song of the prothonotary warbler. These bright-yellow birds are a sign that the riverfront forests are healthy, with plentiful insects and snails.

We traveled farther downriver to check the water quality. I joined a dredging crew from the **U.S. Army Corps of Engineers** where the Mississippi meets the Ohio River. This part of the river is one of the busiest routes in the United States for ship traffic. The Mississippi has many curves that slow the flow of water. Soil and sand being carried by the water drop to the bottom and build up. Crews dredge the river to keep it deep enough so ships don't get stuck on sand bars. Sand bars are areas of raised sand in the water. Dredging is necessary for shipping, but it can disturb and destroy fish and wildlife habitats.

A dredge on the Mississippi

Sightings

Red-headed woodpecker

We saw a few red-headed woodpeckers in the refuge. These birds eat insects, as well as fruit, nuts, and seeds.

17

Field Journal: Days 26–27

Kentucky Bend ↘

Seasonal flooding in 2010 and 2011 was the worst in 100 years. Twenty-one people died in Tennessee, and flooding in Nashville caused $3 billion in damage.

Kentucky Bend to North of Memphis, Tennessee

I'm amazed at how the Mississippi River is always being shaped and changed by natural events and human use. Today, we took a small boat around the Kentucky Bend. This is a loop of land called an oxbow. It juts out into the river and separates Kentucky from Tennessee. The Kentucky Bend was created by earthquakes in 1811 and 1812, which shifted the land and the way the river flowed.

I spent an afternoon counting fish north of Memphis, Tennessee. I worked with scientists to make a list of different fish species on the river. We traveled in an electrofishing boat. It uses an electric current to attract fish. We set nets called seines to catch the fish. Our list includes information on the species, where and what they eat, and how healthy they are. The scientists also gather information on the river's freshwater mussels.

Floodwaters cover the land near the river with **silt**. This makes the land more fertile for growing corn, soybeans, and cotton. But floodwaters can also wash away crops.

↰ Electrofishing

natstat STATUS REPORT ST456/part B

Name: Freshwater mussels

Description:
Freshwater mussels refers to mollusks such as clams, shellfish, and bivalves. They filter their food and the river water, helping to keep it clean. About 130 species of mollusks live in the rivers and streams of Tennessee, including the Mississippi.

Attach photograph here ➡

Threats:
Habitat destruction from dredging, and construction projects such as dams, farm pesticide runoff, and overfishing

Numbers: Unknown

Status:
Some species are threatened and others are endangered.

19

Field Journal: Days 28–29

Arkansas Alluvial Plain and River Delta

Arkansas is famous for its rice farms. But today, I visited a farmer who has turned over part of his land to the birds. The farm is located in the Arkansas delta—an area where the river has washed **sediment** ashore to create rich soil. He gave me a tour of the land on his farm that he had turned back into wetlands. To grow rice, farmers must flood their fields with several inches of water. The state of Arkansas paid the farmer to leave part of his land to the birds. Eventually, it became wetland habitat.

Arkansas grows 46 percent of the rice in the United States.

We caught some redear sunfish in the lake and cooked them up for supper. The fish are not only tasty, they also eat quagga mussels. These mussels are an invasive species in the Upper Mississippi River, but not yet in the Lower Mississippi.

We brought the kayaks out again to paddle around Lake Chicot. The lake is an example of how a watershed was saved from destruction. The C-shaped lake was formed 600 years ago. The forests along the riverbanks were cut down for farmland in the mid 1900s. Without tree roots to cling to, the soil washed into the lake. A dam built in 1948 caused more silt to build up in the lake. Fish disappeared and died in the silty water. In 1985, the silt was redirected from the lake into the Mississippi. Lake Chicot's waters soon cleared and it was restocked with fish.

← Lake Chicot is the biggest oxbow lake in North America.

Sightings

Water moccasin

From the kayak, I saw a water moccasin basking in the sunshine. I'm glad it was on land! Water moccasins are the only water snakes in North America with poisonous venom.

Field Journal: Days 30–31

Mississippi River to White River Mouth, Arkansas

We camped at the Dale Bumpers White River National Wildlife Refuge to explore the White River. This river is a tributary of the Mississippi. Several types of trees grow here, including sugarberry, sycamore, and bald cypress. Bald cypress thrives on riversides that are often flooded. Some bald cypress trees are hundreds of years old and can survive the winds of a hurricane! It was amazing to see these big beauties lining the river.

Bald cypress trees in the swampy waters ↓

Wild hogs live in the refuge. They are an invasive species of hog that escaped from farms many years ago. They eat the nests of birds, as well as damage their habitat. ↓

White-tailed deer
↓

This refuge is a swamp forest. It is one of the last remaining forests of its kind in the Lower Mississippi River Valley. The trees grow in areas that are flooded. The refuge has nearly 160,000 acres (64,750 hectares) of trees and habitat. The many streams, **bayous**, and mudholes here are home to thousands of birds. White-tailed deer also feed on forest plains. Our guides told us that hunting is allowed at the refuge. It is carefully controlled to make sure the population remains under control.

natstat STATUS REPORT ST456/part B

Name: American black bear
(Ursus americanus)

Threats:
Forest habitat destruction, hunting

Description:
This small bear lives in forested areas. It eats roots, bulbs, fruit, and berries. In warm areas, only pregnant females **hibernate** during the colder months. The bears were overhunted in the early 1900s. Starting in 1959, Arkansas released 256 black bears. Hunting was not allowed again until the 1980s.

Numbers:
About 3,000 in Arkansas

Status:
Least concern

Attach photograph here →

23

Field Journal: Days 32–34

Poverty Point, Natchez, Louisiana

We took a short detour to see some **prehistoric** mounds of earth at Poverty Point National Monument. The mounds are up to 70 feet (21 meters) high. They are located on Bayou Macon, a tributary of the Mississippi. The Mississippi River and its surrounding area have been home to **Indigenous** peoples, such as the Chickasaw, Natchez, and Cherokee, for thousands of years. About 4,000 to 2,500 years ago, a group built five mounds in the Mississippi Delta. Nobody knows the purpose of the mounds, but it must have been a huge task. The builders would have had to move one million cubic yards (764,555 cubic meters) of earth!

↑ The steps up the mound at Poverty Point

← Today, many Indigenous groups live near the Mississippi, including the Meskwaki Nation.

24

It was hot and humid today. Near Natchez, we rented canoes and paddled on the river. We passed boats full of tourists. Flat-bottomed boats called barges were heading north up the river. Our river guide pointed out that the water has been getting cleaner since a chemical plant closed a few years ago. The Lower Mississippi is muddy green to brown. The muddy color comes from the Missouri River, which adds more silt to the water. We camped on a sandbar and watched beavers swim. A snowy egret stopped by our site.

Tugboats push barges up the river.

Sightings

A number of blue-winged teals dazzled us by the shore. Their dappled bodies contrast with the bright blue of their upper wings.

Blue-winged teal

The Mississippi River and floodplain is a temporary or permanent home to many living things:

25 percent of all fish species in North America

40 percent of the migratory water birds in the United States

60 percent of all North American birds

25

Field Journal: Days 35–37

New Orleans, Louisiana, to the Gulf of Mexico

The last leg of our research trip brought us to the swamps. We paddled our kayaks through the murky water and kept watch for alligators. The cypress and tupelo trees here are amazing. Moss clings to them like a blanket. Swamps act like a giant sponge during floods. This is especially helpful during a hurricane. Swamps soak up rainwater and act as a barrier to some flooding.

Mississippi Waters

Narrowest width:
20–30 feet
(6–9 m)

Widest width:
11 miles
(17 km)

Shallowest depth:
Less than three feet
(1 m)

Deepest depth:
200 feet
(60 m)

BE AWARE

GULF STURGEON

Boaters have been seriously injured from impacts with these jumping fish.

Large sturgeon jump in the river during the summer and fall months.

REDUCE SPEED TO REDUCE RISK OF IMPACT!

Sturgeon can grow to 8 feet and weigh up to 200 pounds. They are a protected species and cannot be harvested. To report sturgeon collisions, call 1-888-404-FWCC (3922).

MyFWC.com

Our boat came within an arm's length of a gulf sturgeon as it "jumped" out of the water. These big fish have plates that make them look prehistoric.

We headed to the Gulf of Mexico with a crew of scientists. This is the mouth of the Mississippi River, where the river enters the ocean. The scientists took measurements of the "dead zone" here. A dead zone is an area where plants and animals die off. The Gulf dead zone is caused by chemical fertilizers used on farm crops. The fertilizers help crops grow. They also seep into the Mississippi and cause **algal blooms** in the Gulf. The blooms suck the oxygen out of the water. Without oxygen, everything dies. Algal blooms used to happen occasionally. Now they happen every summer.

Algal bloom in the Gulf of Mexico →

natstat STATUS REPORT ST456/part B

Name: American alligator (Alligator mississippiensis)	**Threats:** Habitat destruction with the draining of swamps
Description: The American alligator is the largest reptile in North America. It has a round snout and webbed feet. It can range in size from 10–15 feet (3–4.5 meters). American alligators live in rivers, bayous, marshes, swamps, and ponds.	**Numbers:** 5 million in southeast USA
	Status: Placed on the endangered species list in 1967. Today they are least concern.

Attach photograph here →

Final Report

REPORT TO:

BIG RIVER PROTECTION NETWORK

OBSERVATIONS

The Mississippi is an incredible river—winding, diverse, and with a deep history. It is also constantly changing. So many things affect the river's health. Some of the more recent issues have been human-made. The river's floodplain has been altered to fit human needs. Some of the alterations have been caused by dams built to make shipping possible in the Upper Mississippi. Others have been caused by farming and settlements such as cities along the river. I've noticed that flood-protection measures, such as levees, have also reshaped the floodplain.

The Mississippi in Illinois

28

It is a constant challenge to control the river and its sandbars, levees, dams, and spillways.

FUTURE CONCERNS

Hundreds of years ago, farms and cities near the river were small. Today, they are large and numerous. Modern cities have streets that pave over the soil that would have absorbed rain and floodwater. Farms are large operations that use chemical fertilizers. These fertilizers wash off into the watershed and are brought downstream in the Gulf of Mexico. Global warming has changed the climate. Storms are now more severe and more frequent. In turn, this makes flooding more intense. The water flowing downstream will lead to more frequent and larger dead zones. Dredging has made it possible for the river to become a major shipping route. But dredging also disturbs fish and wildlife habitats. Shipping also brings more invasive species into the Mississippi River system.

CONSERVATION PROJECTS

Conservation programs have rebuilt river islands. Habitat protection schemes have made things better for migrating birds and endangered animals. Farmers are being encouraged to make bird habitats. There is still much more to do, though. To prevent harmful algal blooms in the Gulf, farmers upriver will have to build better drainage ditches. This will help prevent fertilizer runoff from reaching the river. We are only now realizing how important swamps are in preventing flooding. We are also learning that some flood protection methods such as dams and levees might actually make floods worse by disrupting the flow of the river. Flood stages then become higher. We have altered the river and changed the landscape to suit us. But in the end, the river almost has a mind of its own. It is slowly altering its own course.

Bald eagle

29

Your Turn

✴ Do you live on or near a river? Or, do you know what watershed you live on? You can do your own river or watershed report! Do some Internet research on a river near you. Or check out your local library. Ask a librarian to help you research your river or determine your watershed. How long is your local river? Does it have tributaries? How was it named? Are there any farms or industries that use the river for water or transportation? Write your findings in your report.

✴ Many river plants and animals need a healthy ecosystem to live. Think of ways you can ensure that rivers are healthy. One way is to conserve water. You can do simple things such as not letting the tap run when you brush your teeth. Or you can use buckets and pails to collect rainwater for gardens and plants.

✴ Millions of people get their drinking water from the Mississippi River. Do you know where your drinking water comes from? What about the water that is used when you flush the toilet? Ask an adult to help you do some Internet research on drinking water. You can also help your watershed by learning how to be water aware. The next time you walk in your neighborhood, count the storm drains. Note where they are located.

Learning More

BOOKS

Where Is the Mississippi River? by Dina Anastasio (Penguin Workshop, 2017)

The Mississippi, America's Mighty River by Robin Johnson (Crabtree, 2010)

The Adventures of Huckleberry Finn by Lloyd Jones (based on a story by Mark Twain) (Usborne Books, 2015)

WEBSITES

www.epa.gov/ground-water-and-drinking-water/drinking-water-activities-students-and-teachers
This kid-friendly website from the Environmental Protection Agency can help you learn about how people get their drinking water.

https://fmr.org
Friends of the Mississippi River is a group that protects the river in Minneapolis and Saint Paul, Minnesota.

http://mississippiriverdelta.org/about/
Restore the Mississippi River Delta helps restore the Lower Mississippi through a number of programs. It performs bird monitoring, tree planting, and water testing.

www.nps.gov/miss/riverfacts.htm
This National Park Service website gives information on the Mississippi River, and its watershed and supply.

Glossary & Index

algal bloom large growths of algae caused when water is polluted by too many chemicals in fertilizer, cleaning products, and sewage in wastewater

bayous marshy areas or outlets of a river or lake

dredge a machine that cleans out an area of water by scooping mud or sediment off the bottom

eroding wearing away by wind or water

extinct when all members of a species of animal or plant die out so that it no longer exists

glaciers slowly moving frozen rivers of ice

global warming the gradual increase in the temperature of Earth's atmosphere caused by increased amounts of carbon dioxide from the use of oil and gas

habitats the natural homes or environments of plants or animals

herbicides chemicals that kill weeds

hibernate to spend the winter in a dormant state

Indigenous people who are native to an area

invasive species plants and animals that are not natural to an area

migration the seasonal movement of animals from one area to another, in spring and fall

native born or naturally occurring in a particular area

plankton microscopic living things in water, often eaten by fish and other animals

prehistoric from a time thousands of years ago, before written record began

refuges shelters or safe places

sediment dirt, soil, and sand that is carried by water and deposited on the land or at the bottom of the river

silt fine sand, clay, or rock particles that are carried by running water

U.S. Army Corps of Engineers a government agency that looks after the design, construction, and maintenance of big projects such as dams, power plants, and canals